HAPPY

by Kerry Dinmont

The Child's World®
childsworld.com

Published by The Child's World®
1980 Lookout Drive • Mankato, MN 56003-1705
800-599-READ • www.childsworld.com

Photographs ©: Shutterstock Images, cover,
1, 4, 8, 10, 14, 22 (top right), 22 (bottom left);
ESB Professional/Shutterstock Images, 5,
6; iStockphoto, 9, 22 (bottom right); Wave
Break Media/Shutterstock Images, 13,
16, 20; Den Kuvaiev/iStockphoto, 15; MN
Studio/Shutterstock Images, 19; Michael
Jung/Shutterstock Images, 22 (top left)

Design Elements: Shutterstock Images

Copyright © 2019 by The Child's World®
All rights reserved. No part of this book
may be reproduced or utilized in any
form or by any means without written
permission from the publisher.

ISBN Hardcover: 9781503828094
ISBN Paperback: 9781622434695
LCCN: 2018944231

Printed in the United States of America
PA02395

ABOUT THE AUTHOR

Kerry Dinmont is a children's book author who enjoys art and nature. She lives in Montana with her two Norwegian elkhounds.

CONTENTS

LILLY IS HAPPY

Lilly's mom was gone on a trip. Lilly missed her. But now Lilly is happy. Her mom comes home today!

Lilly gives her mom a big hug when she gets home. Her mom gives Lilly a gift she bought on the trip. Lilly **smiles**. She is happy her mom is home.

BEING HAPPY

Many things make people happy. Having sleepovers might make someone happy. Some people are happy when they give or get gifts. Playing sports can also make people happy.

Everyone feels happy sometimes.
People may talk about what
makes them happy.

Being happy makes you feel good. It can make you smile or laugh. If you are very happy, you may want to jump up and down.

THINK ABOUT IT

Can you think of a time when you were happy?

SHARING HAPPINESS

Share with others when you are happy. Many people will be happy with you. Tell them why you are happy.

When someone is happy, try to be happy too. It is fun to be happy with someone. Being happy is **healthy**.

Sometimes you might feel happy. But your friend does not. That is okay. Be **kind** to your friend.

20

Sometimes others are happy, but
you are not. Do not try to take
away other people's happiness.
But it is okay if you cannot be happy.
Sometime you will feel happy again.

WHO IS HAPPY?

Can you tell who is happy? Turn to page 24 for the answer.

A

B

C

D

GLOSSARY

healthy (HEL-thee) Something that is healthy is good for the body. Being happy is healthy.

kind (KIND) To be kind means to be nice to other people and care about what is good for them. Be kind if your friend cannot be happy with you.

smiles (SMYLZ) Smiles are a facial movements where the mouth curves up. She smiles when she is happy.

TO LEARN MORE

Books

Allen, Kathryn Madeline. *Show Me Happy*.
Chicago, IL: Albert Whitman & Company, 2015.

Dinmont, Kerry. *Sad*. Mankato, MN: The Child's World, 2019.

Williams, Pharrell. *Happy!* New York, NY: G. P. Putnam's Sons, 2015.

Web Sites

Visit our Web site for links about happiness:
childsworld.com/links

Note to Parents, Teachers, and Librarians: We routinely verify our Web links to make sure they are safe and active sites. So encourage your readers to check them out!

INDEX